Lindisfarne Priory

Joanna Story

Introduction

Cut off from the mainland at twice-daily high tides, Lindisfarne feels today like a remote place. Yet its semi-detached character made the island an ideal base for the 7th-century Irish missionaries, led by St Aidan, who founded the first monastery here in AD 635. From Holy Island – as it came to be known – they set out to convert the northern Anglo-Saxons from paganism to Christianity. Their monastery rapidly became a renowned centre of Christian life and learning, where many treasures, including the Lindisfarne Gospels, were created by the monks.

From the 670s Lindisfarne was also the home of Cuthbert, the most famous of its monk-bishops. After 698, when his body was enshrined before the high altar of the church, Lindisfarne became the most important pilgrimage centre in the north. But this fame also attracted hostile attention, and in 793 Viking raiders began a series of attacks on the monastery that eventually forced the monks to flee to safety on the mainland, taking St Cuthbert's relics with them.

For centuries memories of St Cuthbert and of Northumbria's Golden Age were kept alive. In the 12th century monks from the priory of Durham, where St Cuthbert's body had been enshrined, re-established a religious community on Lindisfarne and built a magnificent new church over the spot where they believed St Cuthbert had once been buried. Though the priory's fortunes were badly affected by border warfare in the 14th century, a small community survived here until 1537.

The extensive ruins we see today are those of the 12th-century priory, and enough of the church still stands – including the extraordinary rainbow arch, one of the ribs from the vault over the crossing that miraculously survived the fall of the tower – for us to imagine its former grandeur.

Above: An initial 'P' from the Lindisfarne Gospels, created here in the 8th century

Facing page: The interior of the church nave, looking west from beneath the rainbow arch
Previous page: The western entrance to the priory church

Tour of the Priory

The remains visible here today are those of the 12th-century priory established by monks from the cathedral priory of Durham. These buildings probably stand on the site of the Anglo-Saxon monastery founded in the 7th century. By exploring the church and monastic buildings, we can attempt to reconstruct what life may have been like for the monks who were guardians of this remote outpost of Durham's empire.

FOLLOWING THE TOUR

The tour of the priory begins at the church, then continues round the monastic buildings (page 13) and concludes with a walk around the area surrounding the priory (page 18). The numbers placed beside the headings highlight key points on the tour, and correspond with the small numbered plans in the margins and the reconstruction drawing on page 12.

TWO CHURCHES

The path from the visitor centre into the grounds of the priory is a good place from which to view the two medieval churches that lie ahead of you. The church on the right is dedicated to St Mary and is in use today as the parish church for Lindisfarne; it dates mostly from the 13th century but also contains 12th-century masonry. The church on the left is the ruined priory of Lindisfarne, constructed by monks from Durham between about 1125 and 1150 in honour of St Cuthbert. Unusually for a monastery, its buildings were fortified in the mid 14th century to protect them from Scottish raids. After the priory's suppression in 1537 the buildings gradually fell into decay.

Notice how the two churches are aligned end to end with each other. This unusual arrangement is characteristic of many Anglo-Saxon monasteries. The alignment suggests that the two churches stand roughly on the sites of Anglo-Saxon predecessors and that you are now near the centre of the early monastery. Although nothing now remains of the buildings of the Anglo-Saxon monastery above ground, there is a large stone socket-base for a monumental cross between the two churches. This may be of Anglo-Saxon date, and in its original position. The domestic buildings of the Anglo-Saxon monastery would probably have been clustered nearby.

This continuity of site is no coincidence. Although the body of St Cuthbert has lain almost continually at Durham since 995, every place at which it had ever rested was considered to belong by right to the community that cared for it. Cuthbert had been a bishop at Lindisfarne and was buried here in 687; 11 years later, in 698, his remains – miraculously preserved – were moved to a shrine at the high altar within the church. For the Durham monks this spot remained holy, and so they built their new church over the place where they believed Cuthbert had been buried more than 400 years earlier, erecting a cenotaph, or empty tomb, to honour his gravesite. The medieval veneration for Cuthbert is the key to understanding the buildings of the priory.

Above: St Cuthbert with otters at his feet, from a 12th-century manuscript. Many of his miracles were linked with the wild animals, birds and sea creatures of the Northumbrian coast

Left: Lindisfarne Priory viewed from the north-west, showing the alignment of the two churches

Facing page: Detail from a painting by Samuel Grimm of the nave south arcade in 1778, before its collapse. In the 18th century many antiquarians and artists visited Lindisfarne and made careful architectural records of the buildings

◼ WEST FRONT EXTERIOR

The west front of the church was a grand architectural showpiece. It was originally flanked on both sides by tall corner turrets, intended to recall the twin-towered façades common in larger cathedral churches. That on the right-hand (south) side survives, rising nearly to the full height of the building. Battlements were added in the mid 14th century when the whole priory was fortified in response to the outbreak of war with the Scots

Below: A reconstruction of the west front of the church in about 1150

Bottom: The west front today

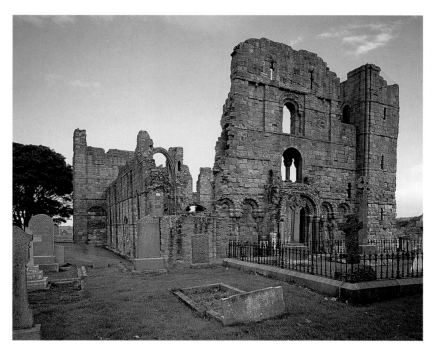

(see page 14). Both turrets contained spiral staircases leading to the upper parts of the church and the roof. The entire façade was divided into horizontal bands by string courses, and the lowest band is decorated with a blind arcade.

The main entrance to the priory church is through the central doorway in the west front. This is set in a shallow porch which is richly carved with diamond and chevron patterns; these contrast with the slim columns topped by simple capitals found on both the outside and inside of the doorway. Above the west door is an opening that originally gave access to a tiny room in the gable above the porch, and above that is another round-headed window. The highest level of the west front is pierced by two cross-shaped arrowloops inserted as part of the mid 14th century fortifications, showing that the building needed to be defended by armed soldiers.

The stone used for the church is fine-grained pink sandstone, quarried locally. Over the centuries this has eroded in some places to create delicate honeycombs in the masonry. Its vivid colour contrasts with the grey stone used for the domestic buildings of the monastery.

LAYOUT OF THE CHURCH

The west doorway leads into the nave, the main body of the church.

The church is built in the shape of a cross: its arms meet under the lofty rainbow arch which is visible directly ahead. Beyond the arch, at the east end of the building, lies the presbytery, where the high altar was located.

Until about 1780 the church survived intact, as is shown by drawings of the time. But by the 1820s the central tower that once rose above the crossing, together with the south aisle of the nave, had collapsed, leaving the church much as it looks today. Although the church is ruinous, enough remains for us to see that it was unusually grand despite its small scale. It was directly modelled on the Romanesque cathedral at Durham, which had been founded in 1093, so creating an explicit visual link between the two buildings. The architecture of the priory church provided an appropriate setting for St Cuthbert's cenotaph. It also encouraged medieval visitors to recall the mother-church at Durham where the body of St Cuthbert now lay.

It is clear from the surviving fabric and also from the positions of the doors that the church was designed to be entirely free-standing. The adjacent stone buildings (to the right) that provided living quarters for the monks were built later, in the second half of the 12th century.

WEST FRONT INTERIOR

Inside the church, above the west doorway, there is an arcade of five small arches at first-floor level; behind it is a passage which gave access to the small room over the porch and a gallery over the aisles to either side of the nave. Higher up, just above the large window and jutting out roughly from the smoother surface of the dressed stone, are the remains of the stone vaults that spanned the nave of the church. These vaulting stubs appear to be arranged so as to receive decorative ribs in the manner of the nave vault of Durham, though these are now lost. This was an expensive and innovative technique, showing clearly the architectural inspiration of the new cathedral at Durham. Projecting from the interior wall on either side of the doorway are the stubs of arches that formed the arcades and galleries of the building.

Above the arch of the roof vaults are the square openings of the cross-shaped arrowloops, which were reached from a chamber above the vaults, constructed when the priory was fortified.

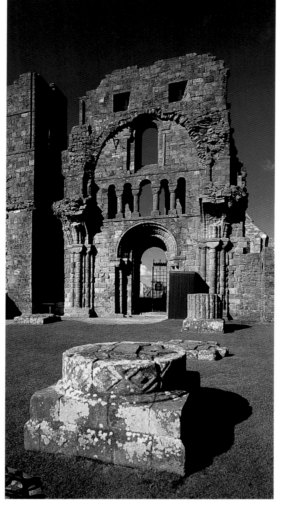

Left: The interior of the west front preserves the outline of the lost nave vault and projecting fragments of the nave elevations

Below: The decorated piers at Lindisfarne are copied from Durham (left), as Samuel Grimm's late 18th-century drawing of the nave at Lindisfarne (right) shows

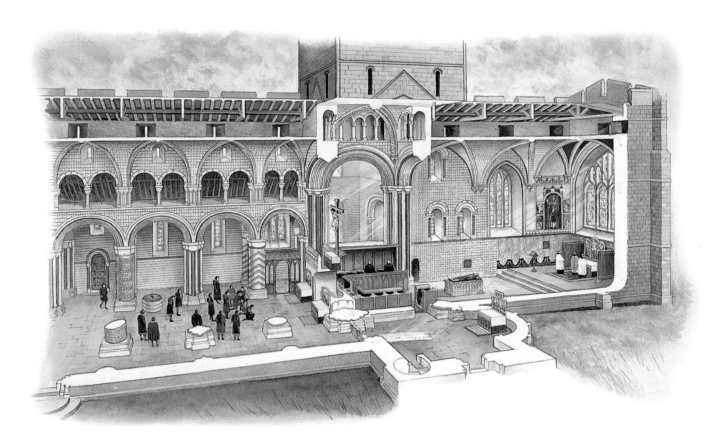

Above: A cutaway reconstruction of the church in about 1500. The monks' stalls were set beneath the crossing tower and separated from the nave by a screen. Before the high altar (far right) is the cenotaph to St Cuthbert

2 NAVE

Moving into the nave, it is clear that most of the south side of the church (to the right) has been destroyed; only the lower courses of the wall and column platforms survive. The north side of the church (to the left) is well preserved. Most striking are the massive piers, or large columns. These are of two designs: large piers with incised geometric designs alternate with those carved to look like clusters of slim pillars. The three piers of the north aisle closest to the west front have collapsed but the next two are complete, with a third forming the north-west pier of the crossing at the centre of the church. Both pier designs are very like those in the second phase of the nave of Durham Cathedral.

The north wall of the nave, beyond the piers, still stands to its full height. A blocked doorway about halfway along, with a slightly projecting surround, gave access to the nave from the north side of the church. There are extensive remains of the stone-vaulted ceiling in the north aisle. The bays between the piers were each lit by a single round-headed window. A larger window was inserted into the easternmost bay (closest to the crossing) in the early 14th century

and some of its stone tracery still survives.

Looking carefully at the north wall, you will notice shallow square holes in the corner of several stone blocks along the wall. These are putlog holes, the remains of sockets for the scaffolding used when the church was being built. Notice how the level of these sockets changes between the blocked doorway and the first surviving arch. This suggests that the church was constructed in two phases. The east end, the crossing and two bays of the nave were completed first; the nave was then extended and the west front built in a second phase.

Many notches and scars are visible in the stonework of the piers and aisle. These probably indicate the position of wooden fittings and screens within the nave. The squared beam slot in the lowest block of the arch adjoining the north-west crossing pier indicates the location of a pulpitum, the screen that divided the eastern part of the church – where the monks held their services – from the nave, where members of the lay congregation and secular visitors were permitted to worship. The pulpitum would have had altars on either side of a central door and perhaps a sculpted crucifixion group above it.

◼3 CROSSING

Standing under the rainbow arch, which spans the central crossing of the church diagonally, you can see that the arch is a rib from the high crossing vault, which survived when the central tower collapsed in the late 18th century.

High up in the crossing piers, on either side of the arch, are the openings of the arcaded passageway that led around the four sides of the tower beneath the crossing vault. Above this rose the central tower of the church. Late medieval records suggest that there were three bells here, as well as a smaller 'alarm bell' to sound in times of trouble.

The crossing, at the heart of the church, was reserved for the monks: this was where their choir stalls, or wooden seats, were placed and where they sat for the monastic services held in the church eight times each day (see page 35). At its height in the later 12th and 13th centuries, Lindisfarne Priory was probably home to about 10 monks, whose days were regulated by the rituals of prayer and liturgy, starting every day with the dawn service of Matins, and ending with night prayers at Compline.

◼4 NORTH TRANSEPT

The northern arm, or transept, of the church, to the left, still survives to the height of its vault. A projecting staircase in its north-west corner, now closed by an iron gate, led to the upper levels of the church. The battlements of the 14th-century fortifications rise above it.

On the floor of the transept is a large block of stone, carved with interlace decoration, which has a rectangular socket in the top. This is the base of a free-standing cross similar to those now in the museum. It probably dates from the period 775–850, and is not in its original position: it was found (in two pieces) during excavations in 1916, having been reused in the foundations of the crossing piers in the early 12th century.

The north transept has another curious feature. There is a short passageway behind the north-east crossing pier that links the semicircular apse (east end) of the north transept with the presbytery. It seems to have been a later modification to the original layout of the church, perhaps when the presbytery was extended in the later 12th century or in response to changes in the layout of the monks' stalls in the crossing.

Left: The north nave arcade
Below: A 10th-century cross-shaft from Lindisfarne, of the kind that would have stood on the cross base now in the north transept. The central figure may represent Christ in Judgement

5 SOUTH TRANSEPT

The plan of the south transept mirrors that of the north. The projecting apses in both transepts would have housed side altars at which the monks said mass daily. A doorway in the southern wall of the transept leads out of the church into the domestic quarters of the priory. To the right of the door are the remains of a spiral staircase that gave access to the upper storeys of the church, just like the corner staircase in the north transept. The staircase was probably modified in the 13th century to form night stairs which enabled the monks to enter the church for the night services directly from their dormitory.

6 PRESBYTERY

Moving into the east end of the church, you will see that the style of the windows changes from the rounded arches and geometric decoration of 12th-century design to the pointed arches and simple mouldings of windows inserted in the 14th century.

In the ground are the foundations of the first, early 12th-century presbytery apse. This was demolished later in the 12th century when the presbytery was doubled in length and finished with a square end. The extension of the presbytery may have been a response to changes in liturgical practices, architectural fashion, an increase in the number of monks here in the later 12th century – or a combination of all three of

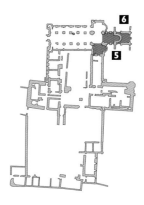

these. At much the same time construction began on the monastic buildings that lie to the south of the church.

At the far end of the presbytery are two ornamented recesses, opposite each other in the side walls. The square recess in the north wall was probably a cupboard for the sacred vessels used during mass; the trefoil-headed recess opposite is a piscina, a basin used for washing the vessels after mass. Their positions suggest that the high altar stood at the far end of the newly extended presbytery. For some reason the last bay at the east end is narrower than the rest.

It is likely that the 12th-century cenotaph, or empty tomb, of St Cuthbert was placed in the presbytery of the church built to venerate him, although its exact position is not known. The earliest reference to it is by the Durham monk Reginald in about 1167, but he does not specify its position. Most authorities have assumed that the monks reused the exact spot of Cuthbert's burial in 698. It is also possible, however, that the cenotaph marked the place where his coffin-shrine had rested in 1069–70, when the Durham monks briefly returned to Lindisfarne with St Cuthbert's relics to escape the armies of William the Conqueror (see page 33). Fourteenth-century records suggest that the cenotaph was topped by a painted recumbent statue of St Cuthbert, made (or repaired) to mark the completion of restoration works in the 1370s.

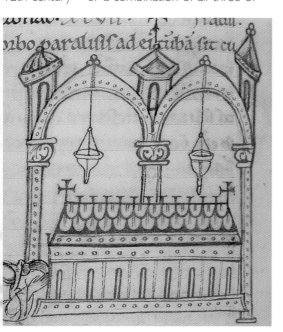

Far left: A depiction of St Cuthbert's tomb at Durham, from an early 12th-century life of the saint, showing how Cuthbert's cenotaph at Lindisfarne may have looked

Left: Looking east from the site of the high altar, with the excavated foundation of the first presbytery apse in the foreground

Facing page: The surviving rib or rainbow arch of the crossing-tower vault, with the presbytery beyond

RECONSTRUCTION OF THE PRIORY IN ABOUT 1500

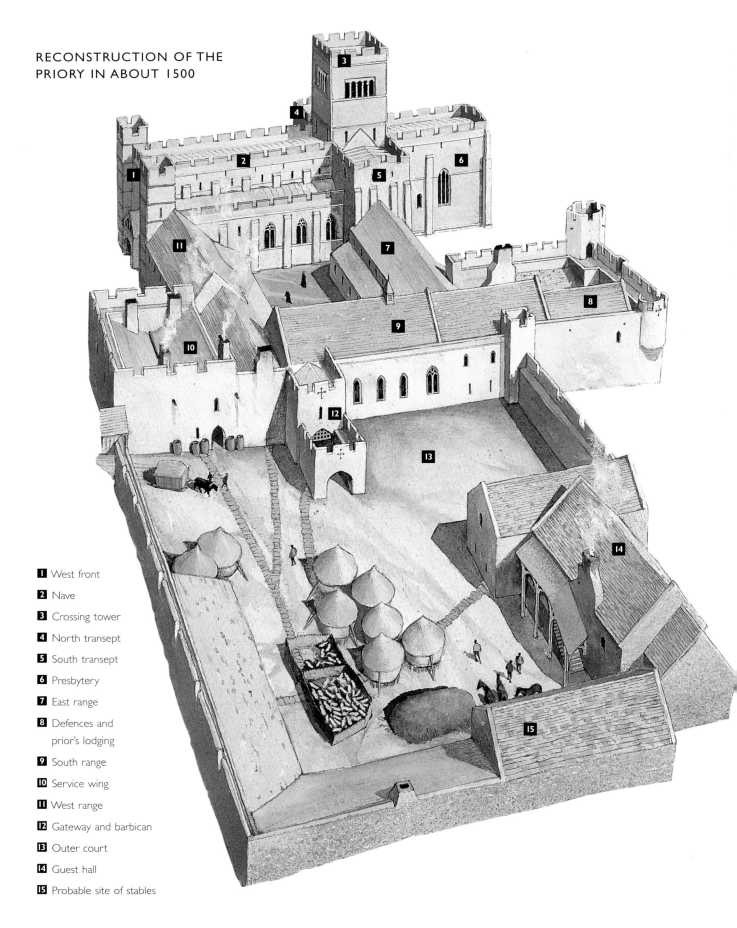

1 West front
2 Nave
3 Crossing tower
4 North transept
5 South transept
6 Presbytery
7 East range
8 Defences and
   prior's lodging
9 South range
10 Service wing
11 West range
12 Gateway and barbican
13 Outer court
14 Guest hall
15 Probable site of stables

THE MONASTIC BUILDINGS

The buildings south of the church formed the living quarters of the monks. The tall chimneystack directly ahead marks the site of the prior's lodgings. Ahead and to the right lie the service and storage rooms, on the south and west sides of the courtyard.

Notice how the colour of the stone changes from the pink sandstone of the church to grey stone for the monastic buildings, indicating two principal phases of construction. It seems that the monks' domestic quarters were begun in the late 12th century after the church had been completed, and for this reason they are not completely integrated with it. This is the reverse of the usual building sequence in a monastery, and the priority given to the church here highlights once more its importance to the community of Durham. The west range (to the right) was the earliest part of the domestic complex to be built; the east range (where you are now standing) is the latest and was built in the 13th century. The whole complex was extensively reconstructed in the mid 14th century with alterations to the hall and buildings of the south range opposite, which came to dominate the layout.

Superficially, the arrangement at Lindisfarne resembles a conventional monastic cloister, in which the main buildings are arranged round three sides of arcaded walkways. But in fact the design is unorthodox in many ways. The emphasis of the monastic buildings here is on the large hall that sits south of, and parallel to, the church. There are no clear signs of a colonnaded cloister or evidence for a chapter house projecting out from the east range. The doors in the south transept and midway along the south wall of the church are also not part of a conventional monastic plan – ordinarily, doors would open from the west and east ends of the south aisle directly into a cloister arcade.

The remains of the monastic quarters surviving here are much more like those of a secular residence than is usual in a priory complex of this type. The large outer court to the south, with its unusually well-preserved perimeter wall, enhances this impression.

Below: The priory seen from a similar angle to the reconstruction opposite, with the outer court in the foreground

The Priory's Defences

The priory was fortified in the mid 14th century in response to war with the Scots – battlements, towers and a barbican were built

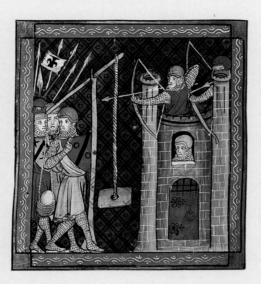

After King Edward I (reigned 1272–1307) invaded Scotland in 1296, the border area, previously peaceful and prosperous, was plunged into a long period of economic depression and chronic insecurity. The income of Lindisfarne Priory, which depended chiefly on tithes and land rents from nearby estates on the mainland, shrank drastically and never recovered. As income fell, so did the number of monks at the priory; by 1344 only four monks remained.

The fortification of the priory was probably begun between the 1320s and 1340s during the Scottish campaigns of Edward II (reigned 1307–27) and Edward III (reigned 1327–77). Battlements were built all around the top of the church and its towers, and chambers were constructed above the vaults with defensive arrowloops, many of which are still visible. The monastic buildings were also protected: a strong wall and tower were built east of the prior's lodgings and a barbican, or outer defence, was added to the gateway between the outer courtyard and the cloister. At the same time, the domestic quarters were reorganised and any sense of a cloister plan was finally abandoned. The west range was largely reconstructed and the hall in the south range rebuilt.

Above: A mid 14th-century manuscript illumination of soldiers defending their fortress

7 EAST RANGE

Of the east range, only the foundations and lower parts of the walls remain. The first, small room – nearest to the church – was perhaps the sacristy, where the vestments worn by the celebrant of the services and liturgical utensils were kept.

The next, long room is where on a normal monastic plan we would expect to find the chapter house, the monks' formal meeting chamber in which they met daily to discuss business, recite chapters from their monastic rule and commemorate their dead. In larger monasteries, the chapter house is a separate building projecting eastward from a cloister; but at Lindisfarne the chapter house – if such it was – was constrained to the width of the east range. The surviving columns, built into the east wall, were finely made, although the ceiling vaults that sprung from them were low. This arrangement may suggest that the room was in fact an undercroft or storage area rather than the chapter house. The monks' dormitory was above this vaulted room; the day stairs to the dormitory can be seen to the right of the doorway at the south end. This doorway leads into the parlour, where conversation was allowed.

The room beyond the parlour is the warming house, which was originally the only room in the monastery where a fire was permitted. The large chimneystack to your left, with fireplaces on the

ground and first floors, was built in the mid 14th century when these buildings were extensively remodelled. The rooms above the warming house served as part of the prior's lodging; access to these upper rooms was via the staircase visible in the south wall of the room, opposite the fireplace.

8 DEFENCES AND PRIOR'S LODGING

The 14th-century accounts for the priory (now kept in Durham) show that the monastic quarters were heavily repaired and altered in the mid 14th century. Around this time changes were made to the layout of the buildings that reflected both a reduction in the number of monks and burdens imposed by the outbreak of war with the Scots. These changes focused on the buildings that lay parallel to the church: the prior's lodging was extended eastwards with substantial defences, the hall in the south range was modified and the service quarters were extensively reconstructed.

The functions of the structures in the easternmost part of the monastic buildings are difficult to interpret. The high, thick, defensive walls rise up all around. In the north-east corner is a substantial projecting tower which provided defensive cover for the east end of the church and the harbour beyond. The other corner has a smaller projecting turret. These walls are the most substantial remains of the 14th-century defences.

Above: The massive 14th-century chimneystack beyond the east range, which probably served the warming house on the ground floor and the prior's lodging above

Far left: A column that would have supported a vault in the east range

Left: An external view of the 14th-century defences enclosing the prior's lodging, with the presbytery of the church to the right

9 10 SOUTH RANGE AND SERVICE WING

The low walls of the south range mark the remains of the great hall. This was originally the refectory, or communal dining room, where the monks ate their meals in silence while listening to readings. It was widened and rebuilt in the 13th century and again in the mid 14th century, when it was altered into a great hall for the prior and the four or five monks who remained with him. This is probably the building referred to in the mid 14th-century accounts as 'the new hall of St Cuthbert'. A raised area, perhaps for the prior's table, is identifiable at the end nearest the prior's lodgings. In the centre is a fireplace. The late 14th- and 15th-century records say that the hall was furnished with four tables, a long bench with red cushions, candlesticks, silver plate, basins and ewers, an iron poker and a tapestry on the wall. At the western end of the hall is a screens passage – a corridor across the width of the hall created by a wooden partition, separating the hall from the service quarters beyond.

Three doors in the west wall of the screens passage lead to the service wing. The doorway on the right leads into a larder. This room has a pit in the floor, once lined with lead, perhaps for keeping foodstuffs cool. At the back of the complex – entered via the central door in the screens passage – are three rooms containing ovens: these were built in the 1360s with thick, protective outer walls. The room on the right, behind the larder, has a circular oven in the wall. Behind it was the brewhouse which has a sink set in the floor and, in the corner, the remains of a kiln that would have heated a large metal vessel hanging above. A kitchen or bakehouse, in the south-west corner, has a large circular oven set into thick walls. A doorway in the south wall led directly into the outer courtyard so that provisions could be brought in easily from the storehouses. The left-hand door from the screens passage led into a kitchen, which has a flagstone floor and the remains of two fireplaces.

11 THE WEST RANGE

The rooms in the west range, between the kitchens and the church, contain several storage rooms on the ground floor. The west range was built in the late 12th century but was reconfigured in the mid 14th when the ground floor was partitioned into three vaulted rooms. These

Above: A monk-cellarer testing his brew, from a 13th-century manuscript
Right: Benedictine monks dining, from a 15th-century French manuscript

rooms would probably have been used as cellars for storing wine, beer and food provisions, as well as the utensils and linen used in the great hall. The upper floor may have served originally as the prior's quarters, and later perhaps as lodgings for important guests. Some rooms may have had other functions, such as an infirmary or servants' quarters, that varied according to the needs of the community.

⑫ GATEWAY AND BARBICAN

Return to the screens passage and walk along the flagstone paving ahead. The southern end of the passage is protected by a substantial fortified gateway, with a barbican, or defended entrance, constructed in the 14th century, projecting into the outer court. About halfway along, blocks of masonry on either side mark the location of a pair of heavy doors. Just behind these blocks are grooves for a portcullis. The barbican extends beyond this – notice how the flooring changes from flagstones to cobbles. A defended gateway is an unusual feature in a monastery. The structure enabled the gatekeeper to control access to the hall and inner courtyard and to defend it if the outer courtyard was attacked.

Above left: The remains of the gateway and barbican, looking north towards the church. The outer door was closed with a portcullis and the passageway lined with stone benches for waiting visitors

Left: Part of the service wing
❶ *An oven, set in the thick outer wall of the kitchen*
❷ *External wall of the west range, before its enclosure by the later service wing*
❸ *Remains of the original kitchen floor*

Right: A medieval sheep pen, depicted in the 14th-century Luttrell Psalter. In the Middle Ages Lindisfarne's outer court probably resembled a farmyard

🔢 OUTER COURT

The outer courtyard and perimeter walls of the monastery are well preserved at Lindisfarne. The buildings visible here were probably enclosed in the later Middle Ages, perhaps to protect key resources during the period of border warfare.

On the eastern side (to the left) are the remains of buildings that may originally have functioned as accommodation for important pilgrims or guests who had business dealings with the Durham monks stationed at Lindisfarne. This comprised an upper-floor hall in the centre, with service rooms to the left and a small chamber at the other end.

The next building, ranged along the far south wall, may have been a stable, with a hay loft above. Beside this was a chamber with a kiln, probably for drying corn, followed by a room with a well and another, in the south-west corner, with the remains of a vat set into the floor –

perhaps connected with tanning or brewing.

In the late Middle Ages the outer courtyard would probably have resembled a busy farmyard, with haystacks, woodpiles and animals, particularly cows, sheep, pigs and fowl. All this enabled the monks to be self-sufficient during the winter months and in times of warfare. The courtyard is likely to have contained wooden structures – some free-standing, others butting up against the west wall – as well as the stone buildings we can see today.

Along the top of the west wall are the remains of a walkway with battlements that formed part of the 14th-century fortifications. These wall fortifications, with the defended gateway, enabled the outer courtyard to function much like the outer bailey of a castle, protecting the core buildings beyond.

To leave the priory, retrace your steps to the west door of the church.

THE PRIORY'S SURROUNDINGS

The high ground to the south of the priory can be reached by leaving the site past the visitor centre and turning left, then left again along the track. Just offshore, between Lindisfarne and the mainland, is the little island known now as St Cuthbert's Island, the site of the 7th-century hermitage used by Cuthbert and his successors as a retreat. The island is accessible on foot at low tide and the footings of low walls (probably late medieval) are still clearly visible under the turf.

Right: The outer court viewed from the south

1 Wall of the outer court, with battlements along the top

2 Ruins of the priory's guest hall

3 Probable site of the stables

The path continues up onto the high ridge known as the Heugh, formed by the same ridge of volcanic rock that underlies Lindisfarne Castle, across the harbour. On a clear day Bamburgh Castle and the Farne Islands are easily visible across the sea to the south-east. The Heugh also gives a good view of the priory across the outer courtyard. Archaeological remains of structures have been recorded on the Heugh, some of which may relate to the Anglo-Saxon monastery. Early medieval monasteries were often surrounded by a wall or ditch, known as a vallum, that delineated its boundary; the Heugh probably marked the southern boundary at Lindisfarne.

Along the Heugh, in the direction of the harbour and castle, you can see the surviving traces of harbour defences constructed in the 16th and 17th centuries. A fort, known as Osborne's Fort, was built on the eastern end of the Heugh in the 1670s. Traces of the redoubt, or central stronghold, of this structure remain. It is rare for a fort of this size and type to survive at all, unmodified by later reconstructions; its importance thus belies its unprepossessing appearance. On the far side of the harbour is Lindisfarne Castle, which dates originally from the 1540s and is built on the easternmost point of the ridge of volcanic rock.

The path continues diagonally across the field back towards the priory and provides a good view of the 14th-century fortifications of the church and its buildings.

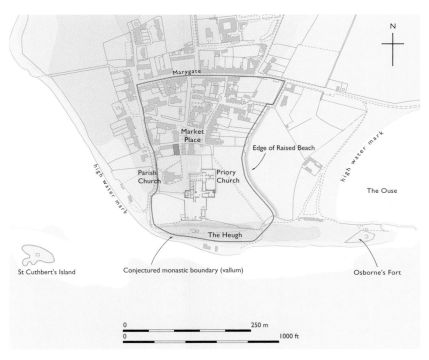

Top: Lindisfarne Castle, with the remains of Osborne's Fort in the foreground
Above: The priory's surroundings, showing the probable line of the vallum or monastic boundary
Left: St Cuthbert's Island

History

The history of Lindisfarne is that of two monasteries. The first, established in AD 635 by Aidan at the invitation of King Oswald of Northumbria, became one of the most important centres of early Christian life and learning, but was abandoned in 875 in the face of repeated Viking attacks. The second was founded by monks from Durham in the early 12th century. The two are linked by the figure of Cuthbert, Lindisfarne's greatest saint.

READING THE HISTORY

This section describes the history of both monasteries, with the history of the post-Conquest monastery beginning on page 33. There are features on Celtic Christianity (page 22), Bede (page 25), St Cuthbert's relics (page 26) and the Anglo-Saxon sculptures from Lindisfarne (page 31).

ORIGINS: ANGLO-SAXON NORTHUMBRIA

Lindisfarne is intimately connected with the history of Christianity in Britain. In AD 635 the Northumbrian king, Oswald (reigned 634–43), summoned an Irish monk called Aidan from Iona – the island monastery off the south-west coast of what is now Scotland – to be bishop of his kingdom. Oswald granted Aidan and his companions the small tidal island of Lindisfarne on which to found a monastery. Thus Lindisfarne became the base for the conversion of the northern kingdoms of the Anglo-Saxons from paganism to Christianity, and one of the most important cultural centres of its age.

Following the general collapse of Roman military rule in the early 5th century AD, Britain became fragmented into numerous small kingdoms. By the 7th century, Oswald's Northumbrian kingdom dominated Britain. Northumbria consisted of two parts: Bernicia in the north, centred on the royal fortress at Bamburgh, 10km (6 miles) south down the coast from Lindisfarne; and Deira, focused on the old Roman city of York. These two Northumbrian sub-kingdoms have ancient British rather than Old English names, suggesting that they may not have come under Anglo-Saxon control until as late as the mid 6th century.

Aidan's mission was not the first to reach Anglo-Saxon Northumbria. In 597 Pope Gregory the Great had sent Augustine from Rome to England with a group of 40 missionaries to convert the English from paganism; he established his mission in Canterbury, the capital of the kingdom of Kent. Oswald's predecessor, King Edwin (reigned 616–33), had converted to Christianity after his marriage to a Christian princess from Kent, Æthelburga. She was accompanied to Northumbria by a Roman missionary, Paulinus, who became bishop in York in 625. Paulinus eventually baptised Edwin in 628 and is said to have baptised and preached to crowds 'who flocked to him from every village in the district'; but his Northumbrian mission ceased abruptly in 633 when Edwin was slain in battle. Having lost his protector and patron, Paulinus was forced to return to Canterbury.

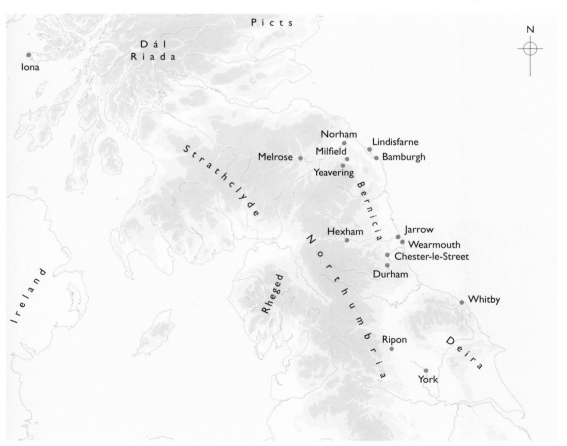

Left: Northern Britain in the early Middle Ages, showing the principal centres connected with its conversion to Christianity

Facing page: Detail of a decorative 'carpet page' from the Gospel of St John in the Lindisfarne Gospels, produced at the monastery in about 700–25

Celtic Christianity

The Irish church evolved along different lines from that of Gaul and Italy, developing its own doctrines and rituals

Christianity came to Ireland in the 5th century. Because Ireland had never been absorbed into the Roman Empire, the Irish church evolved along different lines from that in Gaul or Italy, both in organisation and ritual practices. Rural monasteries in remote locations were especially influential. Whereas in the Roman church bishops were based in towns, in the Irish church bishops were often monks based in monasteries, living under a monastic rule and under the authority of an abbot who was frequently from the royal clan. Monasticism flourished in Ireland with a strong emphasis on scholarship, asceticism, penance and acts of pilgrimage, often expressed as missionary activity.

The most influential Irish monastery in the 7th century was on the island of Iona. From there, missionaries converted the Picts in northern Scotland. Some Irish pilgrims travelled further afield: between 590 and 615 Columbanus established hugely influential Irish-style monasteries at Luxeuil in France and Bobbio in Italy. It was in this spirit that Irish missionaries came to Lindisfarne in 635.

The Celtic church also developed idiosyncratic doctrines and rituals: for example, the style of the tonsure or haircut worn by Irish monks was markedly different from the Roman style. Most significant was the difference in the way the two traditions calculated the date of Easter (see page 24).

Below left: A depiction of a monk with a Celtic-style tonsure, from the 7th-century Book of Durrow
Below right: An early 13th-century manuscript miniature showing a monk being given a Roman-style tonsure

OSWALD AND AIDAN

Oswald's accession in 634 refocused Northumbrian power not in York but further north in Bernicia, around the royal palaces at Yeavering, Mælmin (Milfield) and Bamburgh. Oswald's gift of Lindisfarne to the monks from Iona enabled them to establish a monastery and bishopric in the political heart of the Northumbrian kingdom. The ultimate success of their mission, and the long-term wealth of their monastery, was founded on the proximity of the monks to the royal dynasty of Bernicia.

Oswald had spent much of his youth during Edwin's reign in exile in the kingdom of Dál Riada, which incorporated the Western Isles and Argyll, as well as the north of Ireland. There he was converted to Christianity, and so it was natural for him to turn to the Irish and to the monastery of Iona for a bishop for Northumbria. Iona was not only the spiritual heart of the Dál Riadan kingdom but was also a place of real political influence and a refuge for exiles. Lindisfarne may have been selected for the new monastery partly because it physically resembled the location of the mother house on Iona. The first three bishops of Lindisfarne – Aidan, Finan and Colman – were Irishmen who came to Northumbria directly from the monastery of Iona.

Oswald's first bishop was the monk Aidan. Another had been sent at first but had soon returned home to Iona, complaining that the English had unyielding, barbarous minds and had refused to listen to him. Aidan proved a greater

success and worked closely with the king. Oswald was not only his patron but also his interpreter when he preached to the Northumbrian nobility, as Aidan had an imperfect grasp of the English language; because of his exile in Dál Riada, Oswald spoke fluent Irish. For 17 years Aidan travelled between churches built on royal estates, ministering to the Northumbrians. It was said that he neither sought after nor cared for worldly possessions and that he gave away gifts from kings or rich men to the poor whom he met on his travels. He kept some money to buy the freedom of those who had been sold into slavery; these people became his disciples, and some he ordained as priests.

Aidan was renowned for his frugal habits and asceticism – traits of the Irish church much admired in later times. His episcopacy established Christianity in Northumbria on firmer ground than ever before. From Lindisfarne, monks and priests trained in the Irish ways were sent out to convert pagans, establish monasteries and preach to Christians throughout Anglo-Saxon England.

THE EARLY MONASTERY

For 240 years after its foundation in 635, Lindisfarne was a monastery as well as the seat of a bishop. The monastery was an enclosed community under the command of an abbot, and dedicated through a strict rota of daily prayer and work to the service of God. According to Bede (see page 25), the monastery on Lindisfarne in the 660s consisted of very few buildings – only those that were strictly necessary for the functioning of the community. There was a church and a cemetery but no grand hall for royal guests. By analogy with comparable sites (such as Whithorn in Galloway) it is likely that other small buildings were erected nearby, although we have scant direct evidence for these at Lindisfarne. We know nothing of Aidan's church on the island, but the sources say that he also ministered from a wooden church at a mainland royal estate.

Aidan was buried in the monastic cemetery on Lindisfarne, but his body was later brought into a new, larger church built by his successor, Bishop Finan (651–61), and reburied on the right-hand side of the altar in the manner of a saint. Finan's new church was built 'after the Irish method, not of stone but of hewn oak, thatched with reeds', and was dedicated later in the 7th century to St Peter. Bede records that Bishop Eadberht (688–98) removed the reed thatch from that church, covered the roof and capped the walls with sheets of lead. There may have been two Anglo-Saxon churches on the site aligned on the same axis, an arrangement preserved in the layout of the two churches today.

Below: An artist's impression of the 7th-century monastery at Lindisfarne. The site is enclosed by a ditch and bank, with two aligned churches at its centre

Facing page: The death of King Oswald, who died in battle fighting pagans in 643, depicted in a 14th-century collection of saints' lives

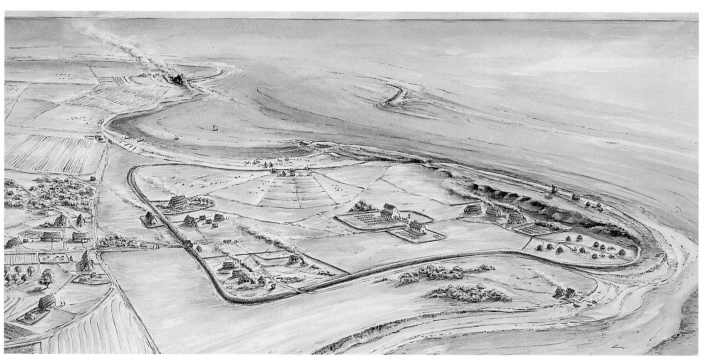

THE EASTER CONTROVERSY

In the 660s, differences between the Irish and Roman churches in Northumbria came to a head over their two methods of calculating the date of Easter, which sometimes produced dates as much as 28 days apart. Since Easter is the pivotal event of the Christian calendar it was essential, particularly in a period of conversion, that everyone was seen to celebrate it on the same day. In Northumbria, the side that won this debate stood to win influence with the king and domination of the whole church.

The problem was resolved at the Synod of Whitby in 664, when King Oswy (Oswald's brother) decided in favour of the Roman calculation. Consequently, Colman (who had argued the Irish cause) and his compatriots who could not agree to this change returned to Iona. The remaining Lindisfarne monks must have conformed to the king's command.

Colman was succeeded as bishop at Lindisfarne by Eata who, at some point in the 670s, asked Cuthbert, the prior of Melrose, to move to Lindisfarne. Cuthbert was eventually to become Lindisfarne's greatest monk-bishop and northern England's most important saint in the Middle Ages.

CUTHBERT

Cuthbert's popularity meant that soon after his death people began to record stories about him, and from these we can piece together the pattern of his life. He was born in Northumbria in about 635, about the time that Aidan came to Lindisfarne. As a child, he had a nurse called Kenswith and enjoyed wrestling and doing handstands with his friends; when he was older he shepherded flocks on the Cheviot Hills above the River Leader. In 651 he rode up to the monastery at Melrose and, leaving his horse and his spear at the gate, asked for admittance to become a monk. He was transferred briefly to Ripon but returned to Melrose, becoming its prior in about 664 after the death of his spiritual master, Boisil. As prior, he used his boyhood knowledge of the local area to minister to the people who lived in the hills and surrounding country.

Soon after his arrival at Lindisfarne in the 670s, Cuthbert began to reform the monastic rule under which the community lived and to bring it more in line with Roman practices. This caused considerable bitterness among the monks and, after a time, he decided to retire and live out his life as a hermit, dedicating his days to prayer and

From right: Three scenes from a late 12th-century manuscript of Bede's life of St Cuthbert: Cuthbert arriving at Melrose Abbey in 651; Cuthbert being persuaded to become bishop of Lindisfarne in 685; the monks on Inner Farne signalling the news of Cuthbert's death to Lindisfarne with torches in 687

silent contemplation. At first he lived on St Cuthbert's Island, just offshore, but later moved to the island of Inner Farne which was yet more remote, though still within sight of Lindisfarne. His life of solitude was curtailed in 685 when, on the insistence of King Ecgfrith (reigned 670–85) and much against his will, he was made a bishop – first at Hexham, and then at Lindisfarne. His duties as bishop brought him back into the world of kings and nobles, and he acquired a considerable reputation as a pastor, seer and healer.

Early in 687, sensing his approaching death, Cuthbert withdrew again to his hermitage on Inner Farne and died there on 20 March, having advised his companions to bury him on the island, out of reach of people who might seek his grave. Bede's account of the death of Cuthbert says that the monks had a viewpoint close to the monastery – probably the high ridge of volcanic rock south of the priory, known today as the Heugh – from where they looked out across the sea to Cuthbert's hermitage on Inner Farne. When Cuthbert died, his companions at the hermitage lit two torches to signal the news of his death to the brothers in the monastery on Lindisfarne.

The Venerable Bede

Bede, a monk at Jarrow, admired the Irish for their spirituality but despised their obstinacy over the 'correct' date of Easter

Like Cuthbert, Bede (673–735) was a Northumbrian and a monk, though he lived his whole life in the monastery at Jarrow, on the south bank of the River Tyne. Unlike Lindisfarne, Jarrow and its twin at Wearmouth had been founded by men who had learned their faith from Rome rather than Ireland. Bede's world was that of Rome: he grew up in the company of men who had been there and brought back to Jarrow many books, panel paintings and holy relics, as well as letters from popes. Although he greatly admired the Irish churchmen for their spirituality, learning and disregard for worldly wealth, Bede despised their obstinacy over the 'correct' dating of Easter. In St Cuthbert, however, he perceived the ideal combination of Irish asceticism and Roman learning. Bede promoted Cuthbert as a figure of reconciliation between the two traditions, since it was Cuthbert who had been responsible for ensuring the reform of the Lindisfarne community to the 'proper' monastic Rule in the years after the Synod of Whitby.

Right: Bede writing, in a late 12th-century manuscript of his life of St Cuthbert

St Cuthbert's Relics

The tomb contained many bones, including the remains of a small man, carefully wrapped in exotic silks and textiles

The oak coffin made for Cuthbert's translation survives today in the treasury of Durham Cathedral, as do objects with which he was buried in 698 and other gifts put into the saint's coffin by later pilgrims. Some were discovered when the coffin was moved into the new Norman cathedral in Durham in 1104, others when it was reopened in 1539, 1827 and 1899. The survival of such a large group of objects in association with an early and well-documented saint's cult is unique in Europe.

The tomb contained many bones, including the remains of a small man, carefully wrapped in exotic eastern silks and woven textiles from Persia and Byzantium. A gold pectoral cross set with red garnets lay on his chest, and beside him were a large comb made of elephant ivory, a small wooden altar covered with silver and church vestments offered as gifts by later pilgrims.

An anonymous account of the 1104 translation records the discovery of a small gospel book.

This pocket-sized Gospel of St John was written in Roman-style uncial script which compares closely with other books written at Wearmouth and Jarrow during Bede's lifetime. The anonymous writer also says that a pair of scissors was found (to go with the comb perhaps), as well as a paten (plate for consecrated bread) and a fabulous chalice.

Another object found in 1104 was a skull, thought to be that of the saintly King Oswald who had died in battle in 643 fighting pagans. Bede had said that the king's head was returned to Lindisfarne and buried in the cemetery. Symeon of Durham, writing in the early 12th century, says that when the monks left Lindisfarne in 875, Oswald's head went too, carefully re-interred in St Cuthbert's coffin. The account of the 1104 translation says that Oswald's holy skull was carefully replaced in St Cuthbert's shrine in the new cathedral. In 1827 pieces of a skull were recovered next to St Cuthbert's body – with a massive, fatal sword blow across the brow.

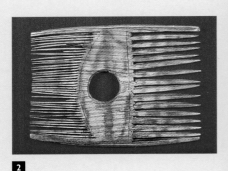

Some of the objects found in St Cuthbert's tomb:

1 Pectoral cross of gold and garnet

2 Ivory comb

3 Embroidered stole, presented to the shrine of St Cuthbert by King Athelstan in 934

4 Gospel of St John in its original binding

5 Part of the silver cover of St Cuthbert's portable altar, with patterns similar to those on the Gospel binding

THE CULT OF ST CUTHBERT

Contrary to his wishes, Cuthbert was buried in a stone coffin within the main church on Lindisfarne, close to the tomb of Aidan. Eleven years later, in 698, the monks of Lindisfarne decided to move or 'translate' his remains from their original burial place to a new coffin-shrine at ground level. When the stone coffin was opened, to their delight and astonishment the monks discovered that Cuthbert's body had not decayed, but was 'incorrupt' – a sure sign, they argued, of his purity and saintliness. This discovery and the translation of his relics marked the beginning of the cult of St Cuthbert, which was to alter the course of the community's history.

One of the earliest products of the cult was the first biography of Cuthbert, which still survives, written by an anonymous monk of Lindisfarne sometime between 699 and 705. Almost everything we know about Cuthbert and his life at Lindisfarne, however, comes from the writings of Bede. Bede wrote about St Cuthbert three times: a prose biography, or life, of the saint, written before 721 at the request of

the Bishop Eadfrith and the monks of Lindisfarne; a version of that text in verse; and in his *Ecclesiastical History of the English People*, finished in 731. Bede was careful to cite his sources whenever he could, both written and oral. A draft of his prose life was read by Herefrith, a priest who had been at Cuthbert's deathbed, and in the preface to the *Ecclesiastical History* Bede also cited the earlier anonymous biography. All these works, which told of the miracles of St Cuthbert both living and dead, publicised the nascent cult of the saint. As such they can be set alongside the Lindisfarne Gospels as monuments to St Cuthbert, to the promotion of his cult and to the rapprochement between 'Roman' and 'Celtic' in Northumbria.

Miracles were soon reported at St Cuthbert's shrine and Lindisfarne quickly became the major pilgrimage centre in Northumbria and a much sought-after burial place. As a result, the monastery attracted grants of land from kings and nobles, as well as gifts of money and precious objects. So successful was Cuthbert's cult that it was to outlast the community's life on Lindisfarne.

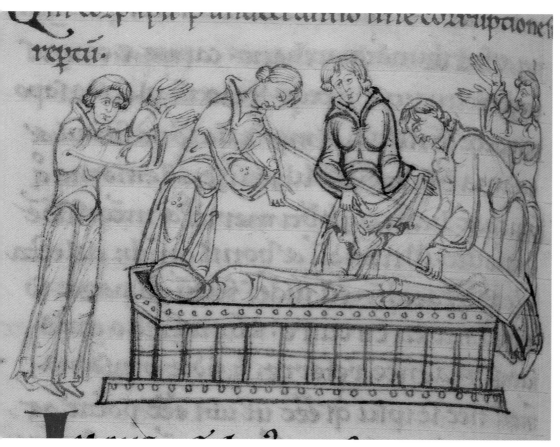

Left: The exhumation of St Cuthbert in 698, from an early 12th-century version of Bede's life of the saint

Above: The upper panel of St Cuthbert's coffin, made in 698, is decorated with inscribed designs showing Christ in the centre surrounded by the symbols of the four evangelists: an angel representing St Matthew, a lion for St Mark, a bull for St Luke and an eagle for St John

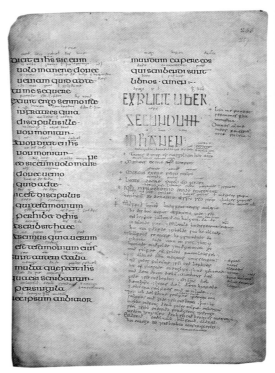

Top and above: A grave marker of about 700 commemorating Beanna, carved with lettering and a cross similar to those found in the Gospels – compare with the cross on the 'carpet page' from the Gospel of St Matthew, above

Above, centre: St Matthew, with his symbol of an angel, from the Lindisfarne Gospels

Above, right: The last page of the Gospels, showing the 10th-century colophon added by Aldred identifying the people responsible for producing the book

Facing page: The opening page of the Gospel of St John from the Lindisfarne Gospels

THE LINDISFARNE GOSPELS

The cult of St Cuthbert helped to ensure the prestige of the community of Lindisfarne, and consolidated its reputation as a centre of Christian learning. One of the results was the production in about 700–25 of a masterpiece of early medieval art known today as the Lindisfarne Gospels.

The manuscript is an exquisite copy of the Latin New Testament. Its 258 pages would have required the unblemished skins of about 150 calves to produce the parchment on which it is written, indicating the substantial agricultural resources at the community's disposal. The book comprises copies of the four Gospels (and their prefatory texts, by 4th-century biblical scholars). Each Gospel opens with a lavish illuminated initial, and is prefaced by a full-page portrait of the relevant Evangelist with his symbol (an angel for Matthew, a lion for Mark, a bull for Luke and an eagle for John) and a 'carpet page' of intricate interlace woven around the outline of a cross. Throughout the book, smaller initials are carefully decorated, and the text is copied by an expert scribe in a script known as Insular half-uncial.

In the 10th century, when the book was at Chester-le-Street, the provost Aldred added a colophon, or closing paragraph, to the last page in which he names the four men he believed had produced the book – the artist/scribe Bishop Eadfrith, the bookbinder Bishop Æthilwald, and the metalworker Billfrith, who produced the metalwork cover (now lost). Aldred himself was the fourth, adding an interlinear gloss in Old English to the whole volume – the earliest surviving English translation of the New Testament. If Aldred's colophon is correct, the Lindisfarne Gospels were written and illustrated by one man, Eadfrith – a remarkable achievement. Recent work on the book confirms this assessment and has demonstrated Eadfrith's astonishing range of innovatory techniques and artistic talent. This was Eadfrith's *opus Dei*, or work for God, made 'for God and St Cuthbert and for all the saints whose relics are in the island'.

The book was made at the time when the Lindisfarne brethren were beginning in earnest to promote the cult of St Cuthbert, after the discovery of his incorrupt body in 698. The Evangelist portraits and the Latin text in this book show close stylistic links with other Bibles produced at Wearmouth and Jarrow in the early 8th century, suggesting a connection with Bede's monastery to the south. Like St Cuthbert himself, the Gospels assimilate the spiritual and cultural influences of Ireland, Rome and the Germanic world of the Anglo-Saxons.

IN PRIN CIPIO ERAT UERBUM ET UERBUM ERAT ABUD DM ET

LIFE IN THE 8TH-CENTURY MONASTERY

By 705 the monks on Lindisfarne lived according to a monastic rule which combined St Cuthbert's teachings with the Rule of St Benedict, written between 530 and 560 by St Benedict of Nursia in Italy. The Rule regulated their days and nights around a strict timetable of prayer and work. Both aspects of their duty were reflected in the physical structure of the monastery and its surroundings, as well as the day-to-day activity of the monks who lived there. One part of a monk's life was filled by reading and learning the Scriptures and by attending services in the monastic church. The other part was taken up with physical work – whether in the fields or copying the holy word into precious manuscripts. Bede was told that, under the Irish bishops, the monks of Lindisfarne possessed few buildings but many cattle – which reveals much about the agrarian base of the monastery. This may also explain why Anglo-Saxon craftsmen there preferred calfskin (over sheep or goatskin) as the raw material for making parchment.

We do not know how many monks lived at Anglo-Saxon Lindisfarne at its peak – about 30 perhaps – but without doubt their numbers were swelled by novices yet to take holy orders and lay people who served the community. These included women, whose names are recorded on surviving gravestones.

During the 8th century, as the fame and wealth of St Cuthbert's monastery grew, it became a place of political influence and refuge. King Ceolwulf, to whom Bede dedicated his *Ecclesiastical History*, abdicated in 737 and lived in retirement at Lindisfarne for 27 years. His successor, the warrior Eadberht (reigned 737–58), besieged the church in 750 (for some reason now unknown), taking Bishop Cynewulf captive to Bamburgh and dragging a fugitive nobleman called Offa 'unarmed from the church, almost dead with hunger'.

Greater scandal was to come. Late in April 793 the monks received for burial the body of Ealdorman Sicga, who was one of the most important noblemen of the kingdom. Sicga, however, had died in deep disgrace – he committed suicide on 22 February, accused of assassinating his king. Accepting the body of a regicide and suicide was a deeply political act for the Lindisfarne community.

THE VIKINGS AND AFTERWARDS

Barely six weeks later, on 8 June 793, Lindisfarne suffered a devastating raid by Viking pirates – their first major attack on the west. For some, the raid was divine retribution: 'Is this the beginning of greater suffering, or the outcome of the sins of those who live there? It has not happened by chance, but is the sign of some great guilt.' These words were written by Alcuin, the York scholar working at the court of the Frankish king, Charlemagne. His shock is clear from the vivid letters he wrote to the Northumbrian king Æthelred and Bishop Higbald of Lindisfarne:

'Pagans have desecrated God's sanctuary, shed the blood of saints around the altar, laid waste the house of our hope and trampled the bodies of saints like dung in the streets … What assurance can the churches of Britain have, if St Cuthbert and so great a company of saints do not defend their own?'

The raid was physically and psychologically devastating: one of England's holiest shrines had been attacked by pagans, and St Cuthbert had not

interceded to stop them. The sins of the Northumbrians must have been great indeed for such a thing to have occurred, Alcuin argued.

The documentary sources, which are very sparse for the 9th century, say that the Lindisfarne monks retreated inland to Norham during the 830s and that in 875 the decision was made to leave Lindisfarne for good. After seven years of wandering, the community – carrying St Cuthbert's coffin and the treasures of Lindisfarne including, it is said, a large stone cross – settled at Chester-le-Street, building a church in the middle of the old Roman fort. Accepting the new order of things, they were instrumental in 883 in baptising a Viking leader called Guthfrith, who was then made king in York.

Evidence survives, however, to show that a Christian community remained on Lindisfarne after the monks had moved south. At least 23 carved stones found here date from the late 8th through to the late 10th centuries, showing that it remained a Christian burial ground. The quantity and scale of the pieces reveal that patrons were still commissioning large sculptures throughout the period of instability when Viking armies were ravaging Anglo-Saxon Northumbria.

Anglo-Saxon Stones

Anglo-Saxon sculptures excavated here preserve many clues for our understanding of the site

Many fragments of Anglo-Saxon sculpture were found during excavations of the priory and its surroundings in the early 20th century. These sculptures preserve important clues for our understanding of the site.

The earliest stones date from the first century of monastic life at Lindisfarne (about 650–750), some perhaps made in Cuthbert's lifetime. Most remarkable are the small round-headed grave markers that date to the 8th century. The designs of the crosses on these stones match some of those used in the Lindisfarne Gospels (see page 28). Fragments of 15 grave markers survive, several bearing the name of the deceased written in runic and Latin scripts. At least one has the name of a woman, Osgyth. Similar namestones have been found elsewhere in Northumbria.

The later stones, from the late 8th to the end of the 10th century, reveal that a Christian presence was maintained on Lindisfarne at a time when the historical sources suggest that monastic life had all but ceased. Many of these carvings are fragments of high crosses, decorated with panels of interlace and animal ornament. The famous 'Viking Domesday' stone, commonly interpreted as depicting the Viking raid on Lindisfarne in 793, actually dates from the later 9th century, and perhaps offers a commentary on the troubled times of the late 8th and 9th centuries as a sign of the imminence of Judgement Day. Many of the sculptures are now displayed in the museum.

Below left: This grave marker of about 700, one of the earliest found at Lindisfarne, bears the name of Osgyth
Below right: An 8th-century cross-shaft carved with interlace animal decoration